# JOHN CORIGLIANO

T0088335

# WINGING IT

## FOR PIANO

*WINGING IT was commissioned by Ursula Oppens in memory of Jacqueline Hoefer*

*The world premiere was given on 5 May 2009*
*at Symphony Space, New York, NY*
*Ursula Oppens, piano*

*A recording is available on Cedille CDR 90000 123*
*WINGING IT: Piano Music of John Corigliano*
*Ursula Oppens, piano*

*Duration circa 14 minutes*
*The movements of this work may be performed individually*

ED 4683
First Printing: February 2018

ISBN: 978-1-4950-9565-8

G. SCHIRMER, Inc.
DISTRIBUTED BY
HAL•LEONARD®
7777 W. BLUEMOUND RD. P.O. BOX 13819 MILWAUKEE, WI 53213
www.halleonard.com
www.musicsalesclassical.com

## Composer's Note:

When I was a kid I was always improvising on the piano. My mother taught piano in the living room of our Brooklyn apartment, and a parade of young people filled the air with Czerny, Mozart, and Bach during my after school hours. After they left, I went to the "big" piano (there were two in the room) and made up things. Sometimes they resembled Mozart, Bach, and Brahms, and sometimes they resembled nothing familiar at all.

I had two piano lessons with my mother. She was a great teacher, but not for me. We fought and I quit. I never studied the piano again, but kept playing it – just for fun. While I don't know the fingerings of all the scales, nor the discipline of repeating something exactly as written (my reading skills were as poor as my digital ones), I did love getting lost in my imagination, and even when I played notes I didn't want, I made them into "right notes" by using them again in the composition (Stravinsky had been known to say that some of his unique sonorities came from his bad piano playing).

Through high school I improvised, encouraged by my teacher, Mrs. Bella Tillis. While both my parents were against my going into music, she always encouraged me – and did for my entire life.

But I had to get serious and learn notation and other musical skills. So I went off to Columbia College, majoring in music, and learned to label the chords I was playing by ear.

Writing music down is a very laborious process. While today's computers make it easier, I still use a 0.9mm pencil to draw every note I imagine. Improvisation is sometimes useful to get material, or to advance a short distance, but since the act of notating it is so cumbersome, it is really impossible to capture an improvisation of any length.

It is possible to tape record an improvisation, but transcribing it is quite difficult, and the composer always ends up changing things while translating sound into notes. I did only one improvisation on tape, the 2 1/2 minute "Hinchi Mushroom Dance" for the film *Altered States.* I was improvising to the picture, and later used the shape of the improvisation (changing lots of notes) to form the orchestral dance in the film.

This project is quite different from transcribing an audiotape. Here, I was determined to improvise piano pieces on a keyboard, and translate them as accurately as possible to the page so Ursula Oppens could perform them in concert. In order to do this, I utilized a computer technology known as MIDI sequencing, which captures both the sounds and a crude but accurate notation of what is played.

I also needed an expert musician and technician to "translate" the notation. This is much more complex than it sounds. Since I improvised freely, there was no steady beat for the mechanism to insert measures. Mark Baechle was tasked with listening to what I played, and then trying to figure out how to put it into measures that made sense. There are many ways of notating the same music, so this required extraordinary musical experience.

Mark made his "translation" of what he heard and saw, and then I often re-barred it, or re-wrote it to clarify the moving voices or the right-left hand relationships. This happened several times until the written piece matched the recorded played one.

Even then, certain changes had to be made – mostly due to my poor piano playing. Repeated sonorities or chords were often not repeated accurately in my performance, even though I knew that was what I wanted. So I had to correct the written proofs to compensate for my splattered notes.

While I tried to accurately reproduce everything I played, sometimes it was not practical. The last piece, a 3 1/2 minute virtuoso piece had ascending passages in running 16th notes in several sections. While I wanted to repeat those sections, I couldn't remember them exactly, and therefore played other 16th notes in an ascending pattern. I could have notated these different passages as improvised, but that would be asking the pianist to play a consistently fast piece that never repeated any notes. So occasionally, I copied the same notes into a later passage that was meant to do the same thing.

The first improvisation was too short, and didn't have a satisfying ending, so I took the liberty of repeating the opening section again (termed *da capo*) and added a single "composed" measure to end the piece.

Other than that, these three improvisations are just that. They are titled by the date they were played.

—John Corigliano

Information on John Corigliano and his works is available at:
www.musicsalesclassical.com
www.johncorigliano.com

*to Ursula Oppens*

# WINGING IT

John Corigliano

## I.  September 28, 2007

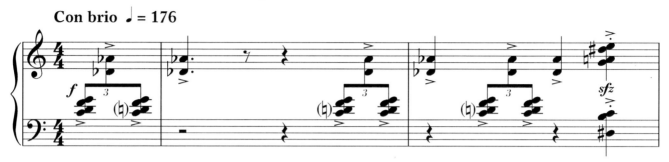

palm clusters

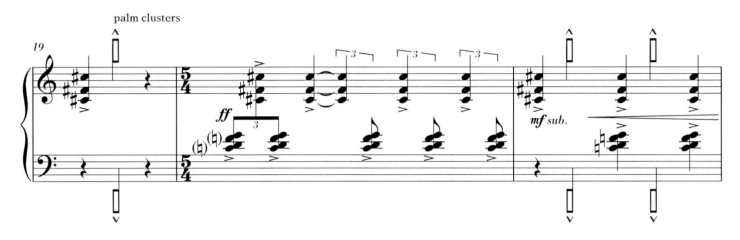

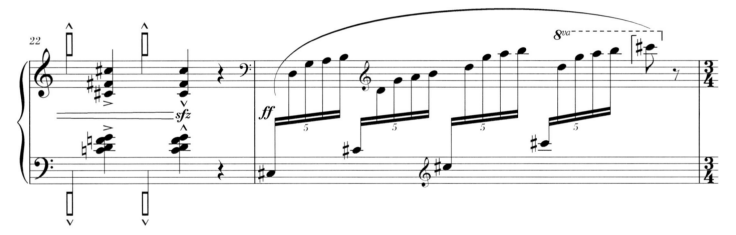

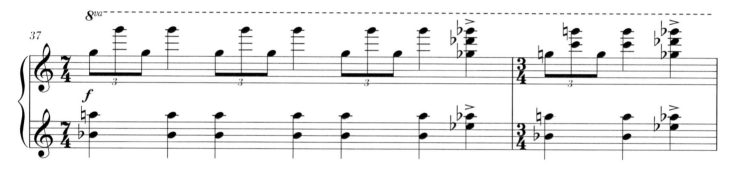

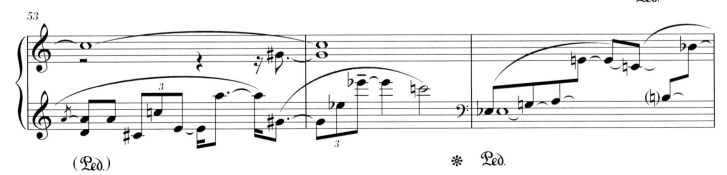

5

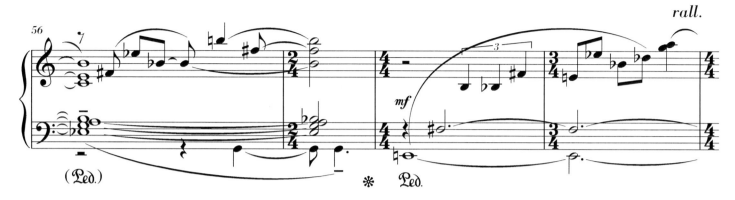

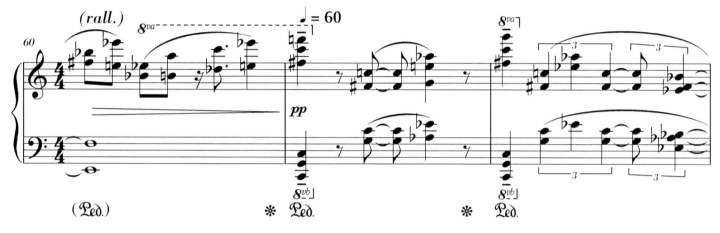

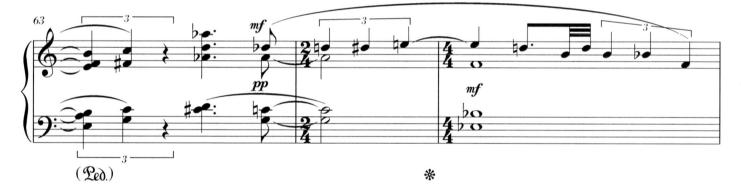

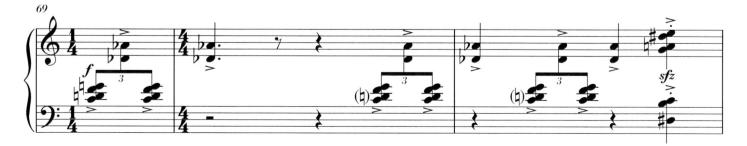

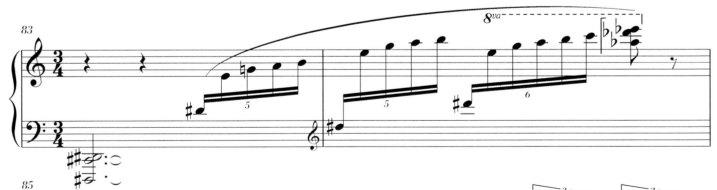

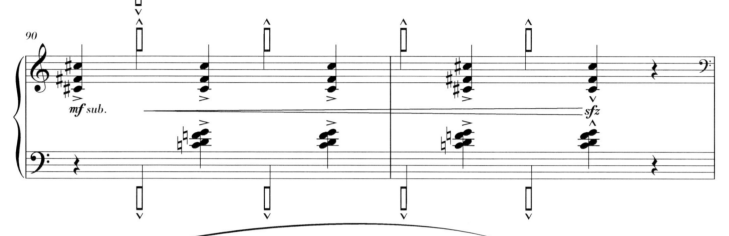

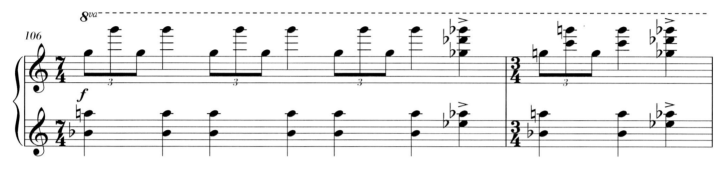

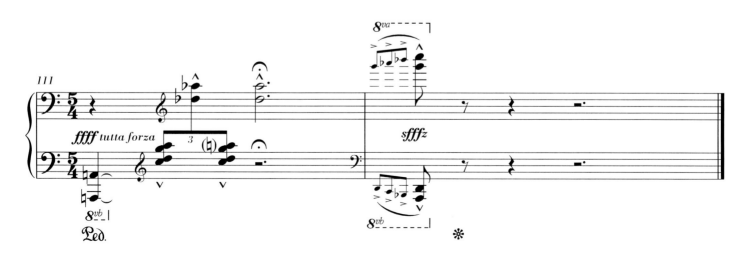

## II.  January 3, 2008

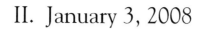

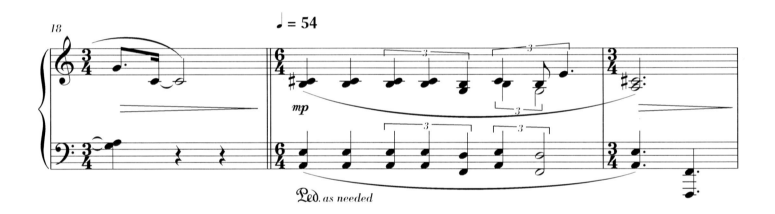

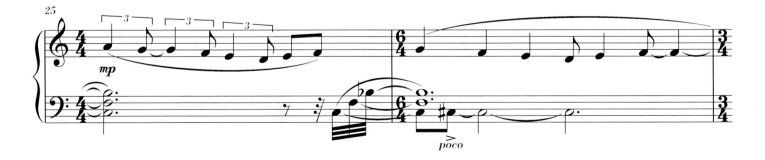

Calmly ♩ = 60 *mp* *ritenuto* *p*

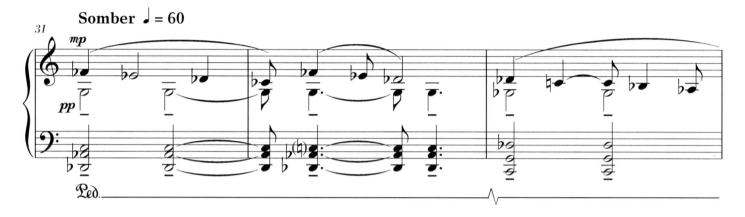

Somber ♩ = 60 *mp* *pp* Ped.

*f* Ped. *ad lib.*

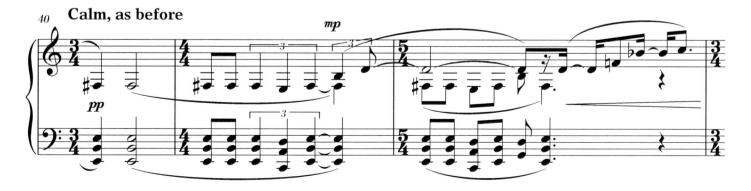

Calm, as before *mp* *pp*

**Simply** ♩ = 46

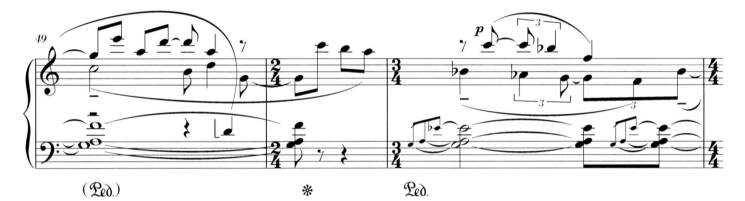

*più mosso* ♩ = 52

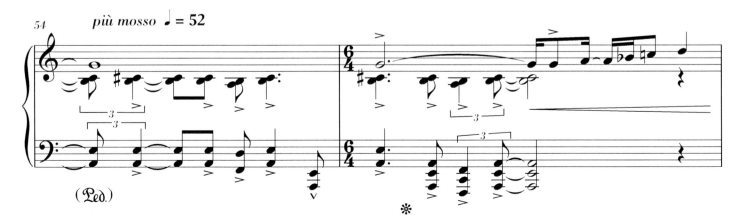

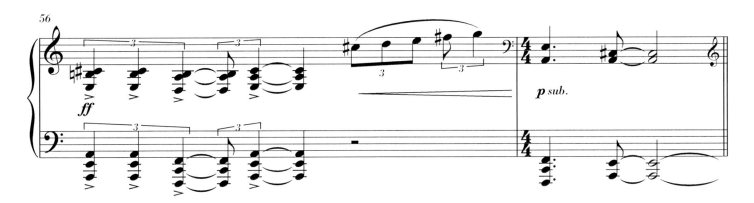

**Moving forward** ♩ = 100

Ped. *as needed*

*accel. poco a poco*

*cresc.*

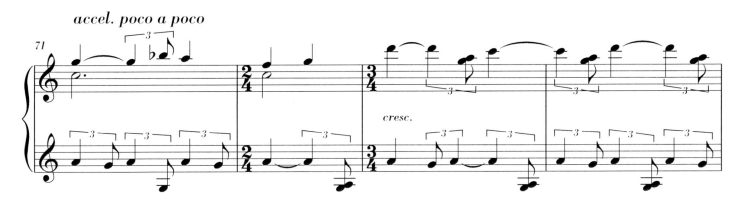

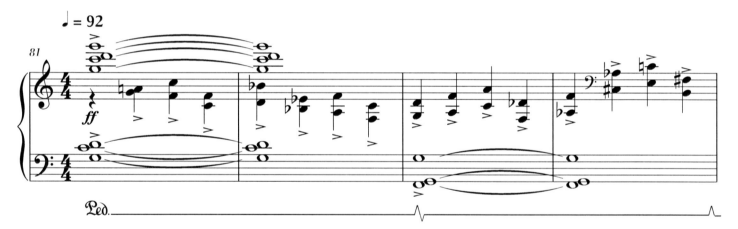

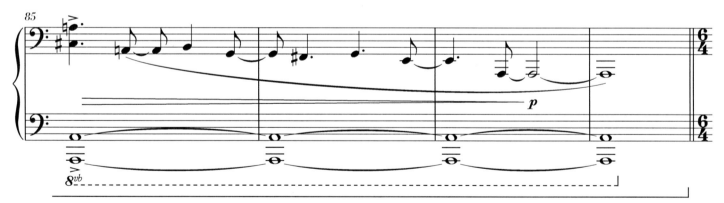

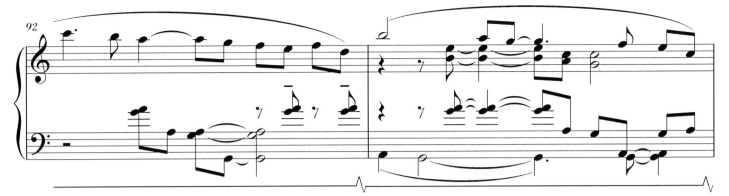

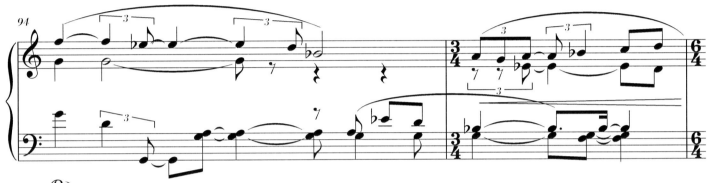

# III. June 7, 2008

**Con moto** ♩ = 120–126

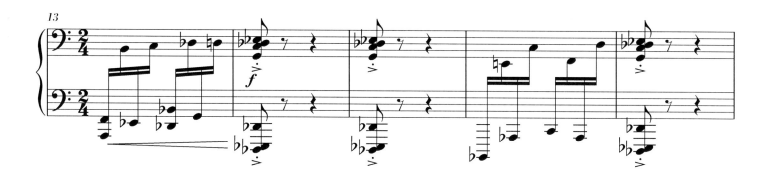

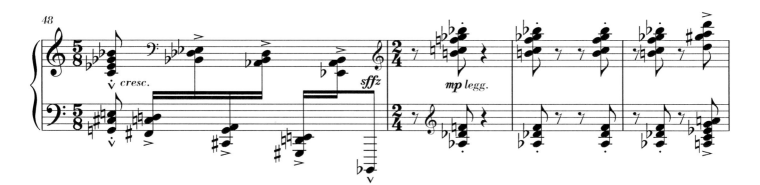

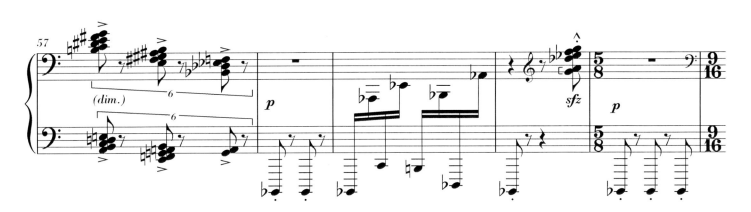

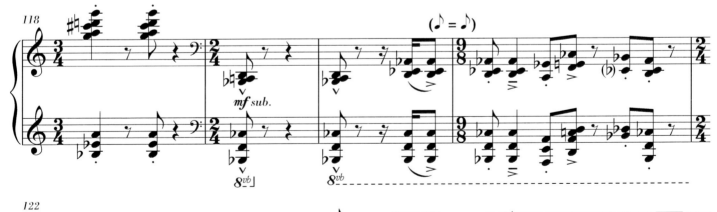

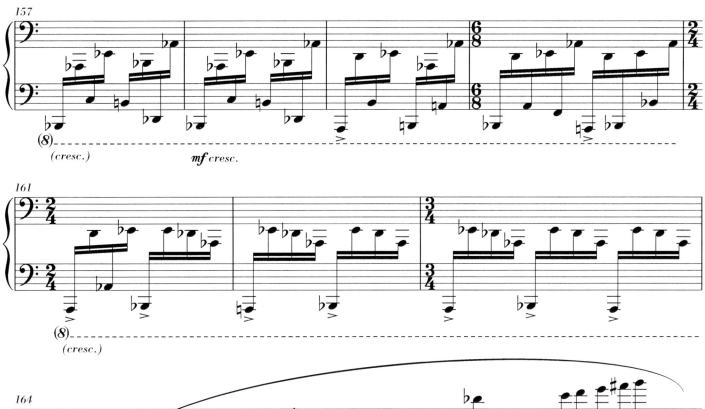

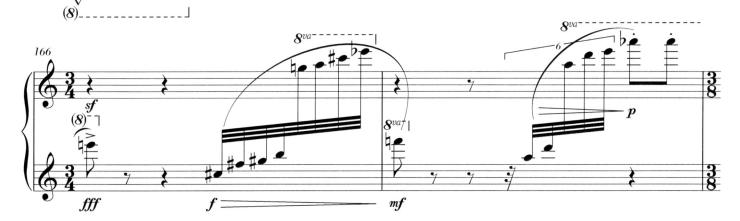